Emotional

Healing

Experience Balance and
Self-Empowerment in
an Age of Rapid Change!

Verlaine Crawford

HIGH CASTLE PUBLISHING

Emotional Healing
Experience Balance and Self-Empowerment
in an Age of Rapid Change

Copyright © 2020 by Verlaine Crawford. All rights reserved.
Printed and Published in the United States by High Castle Publishing

Print Version ISBN-13: 978-0-9998036-6-0
E-Book ISBN-13: 978-0-9998036-6-0

Front Cover Photo from Canva.com
Cover and Interior Design by Verlaine Crawford.

1. Self-Help 2. Body, Mind, & Spirit 3. Inspirational 4. Spiritual
5. Visionary 6. Self-Healing 7. Emotional Self-Help 8. Addiction
8. Depression 9. Metaphysical. 10. New Thought 11. New Age
12. Psychology

I. Title

First Edition

Dedicated to

All those who have been brave and strong
enough to weather the storms and ride the
tides of emotional turbulence.

May you bask in the warmth of knowing that
Love and Harmony will help heal you and your
fellow humans in this time of rapid change.

Table of Contents

Living in an Age of Rapid Change

*How do we stay balanced
in the midst of confusion?*

You have the power to change your mind and experience a renewed sense of clarity, confidence, and self-empowerment to succeed in a rapidly changing world. The key to peace of mind is learning to release the past, relax about the future, and enjoy the present moment without stress or worry.

How can we possibly release, relax, and enjoy when so much that we have known appears to be falling apart? Having to survive when needing to deal with isolation, a pandemic, political unrest, and economic devastation is overwhelming.

Emotional Healing begins with the discovery of the real you, what you believe, and how to establish *emotional balance*. It is helpful to become aware of the beliefs that activate your fears, which are the basis of all negative emotions, including worry, anxiety, and stress.

It is fear that creates imbalance in your life. Fear influences the state of your health, relationships, career, and blocks and camouflages future opportunities. Obviously, we must learn to deal with our fears.

As a lifelong student of psychology, philosophy, religion, and spirituality, I have been a businesswoman and personal consultant for nearly fifty years during which time I have become very aware of how people react to each other and events. My continuous quest has been to understand myself and others and how we interact to establish our perceived reality.

The techniques and visualizations in this book have been used for myself and to help others. They are meant to provide methods to recover from difficult events, to heal, and to move forward as quickly as possible.

In this book, you will find easy-to-use tools, which will help reduce stress and anxiety and release memories of loss and pain. You will learn how to forgive yourself and others, and gain a new perspective on life.

We will explore how the *"The Four Cornerstones of Life"* provide a balance point to expand your well-being, and how the *"Ten Steps to Self-Empowerment"* will begin the journey to recharge your life.

It is my wish that *Emotional Healing* will help you experience a rewarding and harmonious life in the years to come.

With love, *Verlaine Crawford*

Chapter 1

Meeting the Challenges of Rapid Change

The Matrix of Events is accelerating!

For countless generations, humanity has absorbed feelings of fear, anger, and revenge, leading to bloody battles and wars. The opposing beliefs behind power versus subjugation, strength versus weakness, good versus evil, forgiveness versus revenge, and Love versus fear are held deep in the minds and memories of humanity.

These beliefs have now crystallized into an armor of emotions, which blocks the vital energy needed for health and well-being. When statements are made, such as: "I am afraid. I hate that person. My life's a disaster. No one loves me," our vibrational field fills with discord, creating a dense wall of negativity, causing feelings of agitation and alienation. The *mind* becomes *set* on words that create a belief, a *mindset*, which becomes hardened, resistant, and difficult to change.

It appears that our lives are accelerating at a faster and faster pace and that our emotional wellness is being dramatically affected. Forty-two percent of Americans say they can't remember when they had a good night's sleep. What is happening to us as we endure the massive changes taking place?

What is Accelerating These Emotions?

There is now evidence of a change in the electromagnetic frequency. In the last three years, scientists have discovered a significant increase in the Earth's electromagnetic resonant frequency.

In 2017, the scientific community was surprised to learn that the Earth's base atmospheric electromagnetic resonant frequency has increased. The standard frequency of the Earth's electromagnetic field is 7.83 Hz, known as the Schumann Resonance.

In January 2017, the resonant frequency increased from 7.83 Hz to 36 Hz. An increase of more than 400 percent. In the past, any rise above 15 Hz was considered large. According to some scientists, people may experience more stressed nervous systems than usual due to these higher resonant frequencies. As our Planet's vibrational field increases, so will the emotional effect on humanity, causing a global rise in anxiety, tension, and passion.

— InterestingEngineering.com

What happens when emotions accelerate?

As fearful events accelerate, the crystallization that once held our emotions in check is breaking up. People often react more violently. Arguments and hateful words fly in all directions, and the fight or flight response is in full gear.

Part of the emotional outbursts can be blamed on the isolation and devastation caused by the Pandemic of 2020. Another reason is that in our digital world, we base our reality on news clips and social media posts that are often false or misleading, making it difficult to know what is true. Instead of researching opposing views, we adamantly protect our egos and declare, "I am not wrong. I am always right."

We hold on at all costs to what we believe, rejecting any conflicting information that disrupts our beliefs about the ramifications of the "news."

We have allowed the information fed to us to become the beliefs that rule us. Those beliefs are the seeds that magnetize matching frequencies of the people, places, and events that come into our lives.

The result is we often use the weapons of negative emotions to fight for our beliefs, whether the concepts and ideas are based in fact or fantasy. Emotions can heal us or wreak havoc with our minds and bodies. We can choose to disrupt the world around us or decide to live in love, joy, and peace.

Energy Levels for Positive and Negative Emotions

Emotional Energy Levels (Log 200 to 1,000 is positive)			
Happiness Level	**Log**	**Emotion**	**Process**
ENLIGHTENMENT	700-1K	Ineffable	Pure Consciousness
PEACE	600	Bliss	Illumination
JOY	540	Serenity	Transfiguration
LOVE	500	Reverence	Revelation
REASON	400	Understanding	Abstraction
ACCEPTANCE	350	Forgiveness	Transcendence
WILLINGNESS	310	Optimism	Intention (friendliness)
NEUTRALITY	250	Trust	Release
COURAGE	200	Affirmation	Empowerment
PRIDE	175	Scorn	Inflation
ANGER	150	Hate	Aggression
DESIRE	125	Craving	Enslavement
FEAR	100	Anxiety	Withdrawal
GRIEF	75	Regret	Despondency
APATHY	50	Despair	Abdication
GUILT	30	Blame	Destruction
SHAME	20	Humiliation	Elimination

David R. Hawkins

How do we work with these emotions when the world appears to be a science fiction movie that seems to go on and on?

6

Chapter 2

Awakening in a Dream

Thoughts exist as energy
filled with form and shape.

Due to the increase in frequency (or perhaps it has always been true), humans have entered what can be described as a waking Dreamscape. In this Dream-like world, everyone's thoughts, beliefs, and emotions manifest both positive and negative events more quickly.

> *Now our whole life, from birth unto death, with all its dreams, is it not in its turn also a dream, which we take as the real life, the reality of which we do not know of the other more real life?*
> -- Leo Tolstoy's Letters

I am certain most people would agree that living in a Pandemic in 2020 is not a dream. It is a nightmare! We are under house arrest and have started to develop fear of other people and our environment. We cannot shop, restaurants are closed, travel and visiting friends and family is dangerous. This is not our normal way of life. Add to this the fear of catching the virus, a contentious political landscape, the loss of jobs, people without money, schools closed, protests, and strained relationships. Our minds and emotions move from intense fear to anger to disappointment to sadness, and then back to fear.

It is essential to understand how to find harmony in our lives when everything is changing. It is helpful to know the dynamics of how life events materialize into form.

For indeed, you are a projector, a very different kind of projector. You are a powerful manifestor bringing etheric substance into 3-Dimensional form. What you imagine, believe, think, feel, and how you react becomes your reality.

In your waking dream, your feelings are paramount. By keeping your emotions steady, you can think more clearly and efficiently. Allowing yourself to become quiet, you will be able to access intuition that will guide you.

Your thoughts have a reality you do not understand,
and those concepts hold a form of psychic content.
Thoughts exist not as pure energy, but as an energy
filled with FORM and SHAPE.
-- Seth: The Unsurpassable Force of Thought

Thoughts filled with form and shape are gathered from the people around us, as well as the incessant media onslaught that overwhelms our lives, constantly spreading the discourse of fear and uncertainty to increase their ratings and viewers. These negative thoughts form our beliefs and limit our future action and behavior.

Thoughts from our imagination and intuition help develop creative projects, inventions, and concepts about all aspects of life and are invigorated by our enthusiasm and energy in motion (emotions) to manifest a more perfected reality.

So why aren't we creating precisely what we need and desire? What is stopping the flow of thoughts into form and shape for the benefit of ourselves and humanity?

The answer is most of the reality we experience originates in the seedpods of our beliefs. A seed for an oak tree will only grow oaks. Each thought, every statement is a seed that forms a belief if we *believe* it to be true. That belief is stored in our memory and creates a lens through which we see the world. Each person's individualized belief patterns create a screen that blocks out information that may be different from that encoded concept held tightly in our minds.

Our ensconced beliefs separate us and our minds work hard to prove that our beliefs are true. This is the reason we see and react so differently when watching people or an event. Our perceptions (what we see, hear, smell, and feel) all are carefully put through a sieve of our beliefs before our mind registers what has happened. It is fascinating that once these beliefs are established, it is very difficult to change them.

Too many people have been convinced that the world is mostly about suffering, disease, anger, battles, and warfare. Violent people have overtaken peaceful protests and destroyed property in the name of upholding social justice.

9

Might the protesters and rioters use their time more effectively by caring for and respecting individual property and helping those in need to thrive? If we were living in harmony, rather than venting anger and hate, we could concentrate on creating opportunities rather than despair.

Humanity has not yet learned to live together harmoniously. It is time for us to believe we can interact without division, hate, and confusion.

What are your thoughts? How do you feel about your family, community, country, and the world? If you think everything is wrong, it will undoubtedly be so for you. When you see everything as dark and apocalyptic, you are helping to create that reality in your life, in your community, and world.

Can you change your negative thoughts to positive? Is there a way to work with the flood of emotions from friends, family, community, and the world now swirling around you?

Chapter 3

Emotional Balance in the Storm

Is there a way to overcome anger and fear?

Almost every day, we face stress in our lives. Unexpected dangers and rapid changes from nature and the world made by humanity are all happening at the same time. It is easy to become fearful, angry, disappointed, and frustrated about roadblocks that prevent us from achieving our goals.

These emotional responses stimulate a part of our brain, known as the amygdala and the hypothalamus. The signals go to the adrenal glands to produce hormones, such as adrenaline and cortisol, which activate the fight or flight response.

As the vibrational frequency of emotions increases on Earth, it becomes necessary to learn ways to release stress and stay calm amid turmoil and upset. Too many people express their negative emotions in aggressive behavior in their families, on public streets, and on social and mainstream media. Today, there is an epidemic of anger rampant in the world, and it is even more difficult to not respond in the same way.

It is crucial to ground ourselves, think clearly, and remain in touch with Intuitive Guidance to disperse upsets as quickly as possible. What can we do when anxiety or anger takes over?

Here are a few techniques that may help calm down and create balance when we are angry, anxious, or in fear:

- **Stop and take a deep breathe**! Negative emotions create shallow breathing. Slow down by taking long, deep, calming breaths, and try to relax.

- **Relax your shoulders.** When negative emotions take control of our bodies, we tighten muscles in our shoulders and back. Releasing muscles helps quiet emotion.

- **Quit what you are doing or saying.** Ask yourself: *What am I feeling? Am I angry* or *afraid? Am I disappointed or depressed?* Look at the underlying cause for your upset and move into balance with your logical mind.

- **What are you thinking?** Are you caught in a worst-case scenario? Imagine other more positive outcomes.

- **What did the person say?** Is their statement true? Sometimes we don't want to face the truth. Try to understand what was said from another perspective.

- **Go for a walk.** Leave the room and go outside or to another room. Calm your emotions, and clear your mind.

- **Sit down and close your eyes and visualize being calm.** Imagine a lovely scene that makes you feel relaxed. Listen to music that is mellow and relaxing. Clear you mind and listen to your heart.

- **Write down what you are feeling and thinking.** Let the cause of your upset flow through your hands and onto the paper or into a computer. Release all the pent up feelings and see what is bothering you. What is at the center of your emotional response?

- **Is your fear or anger real or imagined?** Look at what is upsetting you and imagine a different result. Fears about the future are not yet real. There are a variety of possible outcomes to any given problem.

- **Drink water and eat a snack.** You may be dehydrated and possibly hungry. Take care of your body for chemical balance and allow you to relax.

You can also choose to turn your words upside down. Change what you are thinking to a positive instead of negative.

- I am **angry and insulted** can become:
- **I can handle this event. I can relax and let go.**

- I am **frustrated** can become:
- **I can move around obstacles and create new paths.**

- I am **afraid** can become:
- **I am safe, healthy, and empowered!**

- I **hate** this person, _____, can become:
- **I send love and healing light to everyone, including this person, _____**

- This job or activity or relationship is so **difficult,** can become:
- **This job, activity, or relationship is easy and fun!**

By switching the words and reversing the intent, you are helping to make a different reality possible.

14

Chapter 4

Visualizing how to Calm the Storm

When you feel upset, angry, frustrated, etc. take a few minutes to go to a quiet room or outside and sit by yourself in a mood of contemplation. Take a deep breath.

Imagine you are sitting in a comfortable chair on the covered porch of a lovely home. You are looking out at a beautiful lake surrounded by tall, dark green pine trees.

You take several deep breaths.

Now project what you are feeling, your anger, heartache, disappointment, rejection, sadness, or stress into the water of the lake. Watch how the water ripples and swirls as it absorbs your emotions being released into it.

Your negative feelings begin to dissolve into the lake. You feel yourself becoming calmer, lighter, and more at ease in your body and mind as you breathe deeply in and out.

With each heartbeat, your breath becomes slower, and the waters of the lake begin to calm, becoming smoother and smoother.

The water is calm. The towering trees and blue sky are now perfectly reflecting in the mirror-like lake.

The scent of the pines move through the gentle breeze, and the stillness amplifies the sound of songbirds in the distance.

You take another deep breath and release the last of your stress and emotion. A feeling of harmony with nature fills your heart and soul as you relax into a suspended state of peace.

You have calmed the waters of the storm.

This visualization is now part of your memory. You can visit the lake and create a peaceful feeling in your heart and mind at any time during your day.

Chapter 5

Isolation and Social Media

How do you use your time?

The Pandemic has restricted families and individuals into isolation or what might be called *house arrest* since March 2020. At the time of this publication, the lockdown in California has been nearly ten months, a very long time to be isolated without physical human interaction.

You may be alone or with a few family members or roommates. But, you can't visit other friends, make new acquaintances, go to work, open your business, go to school, relax in a restaurant, enjoy shopping, go to the gym, or do any other public activity you might enjoy.

Add to the Pandemic the ongoing contentious political climate with the name-calling and uproar during an election year, and you have a perfect storm of emotional chaos.

The truth is that the pattern of our lives has changed dramatically in the last one hundred years. From the rhythmic sound of the clip-clop of the horse's hoof to the double click of the computer's mouse, we are inundated with an overwhelming information flow and constant, rapid change.

At times it feels like the world is unstable—as if it is spinning out of control. Various parts of our psyche are struggling consciously and subconsciously to explain and solve our problems while worrying about our personal life, our community, country, and the world.

The Media Steps in to "Entertain" Us

The smartphone, computer, and television have become our pacifiers to soothe isolation and rid us of boredom. We spend hours watching movies, posting, commenting, and scrolling through Facebook, Instagram, Twitter, and all the other apps waiting for attention.

At the same time, the non-stop information flow has increased our separation from friends and family. Often people place more importance on what is coming through on the internet than conversing with the person sitting next to them. They are compelled to keep checking messages while attending a meeting or walking down the street. They stare at the phone while in a store, at work or school, or even when strolling through a natural setting.

The social media app is free.
We are the products being sold to the advertisers.

As described in the Netflix documentary, "The Social Dilemma," the A.I. in social media apps creates the algorithms that send us the perfect videos and posts that fit our point of view. They choose what we will click on to sell their advertisers' products and services.

What are we doing to ourselves and our children?

We crave attention. We post what we're thinking and feeling, add a photo or video, and then check to see if there are *likes, caring, love, sadness, anger, or Wow*. We diligently read the comments. We hope to receive approval. If not, we fall into upset, depression, or vent our anger and frustration.

The short text messages, tweets, and emails are all unspoken, impersonal communication that wreaks havoc on our sense of self, our view of the world, and our understanding of other people.

For millions of years, humans have been communicating in person. The rule for communication is only *7 percent verbal* and *93 percent non-verbal*, consisting of *body language (55 percent)* and *tone of voice (38 percent)*.

The more we only communicate through email and text messaging, the less we will grasp information from body language and tone of voice. Without practice, we will misread body-language cues. Children who concentrate mostly on social media may have difficulty communicating in person.

We are creating a separate world ruled by the beliefs and distortions presented on social media, which may or may not be valid. The "Techies" have said that fake news shows up six times more often in social media than real, true information.

What does that mean? It means that A.I. is programmed to generate audience response for advertisers, and "sensational" or "fake news" and "conspiracies" do that best.

Each person receives different information.

And, your ever-present digital device is ready to push you even further into your belief system. The apps' designers admit that their algorithms send us each different information based on our reactions to particular areas of interest.

Our psyche becomes distorted because we do not receive balanced information. Instead, the postings and comments manipulate and increase our biases, pushing us to form judgments. We become stuck in a world of misinformation with no contradictions to make us think and question our beliefs.

The constant stream of one-sided opinions and comments add to our stress and discomfort, affecting our well-being. A majority of users have developed a dependency on social media, similar to craving a drug at some level. This high tech drug requires us to keep using it to get an adrenaline hit, no matter if it often makes us depressed or angry.

There are only two industries that call their customers users: Illegal drugs and software. – Edward Tufte

A dear friend of mine, a college professor, shared a story about her students and their smartphones. She instructed her class that she was sending them outside to spend thirty minutes in nature without their phones. They all groaned.

She directed, "Give me your phones and go out on the campus. Sit under a tree, look at the plants, and observe the buildings and sky. Then come back and tell me what you saw and what you learned."

The young men and women shuffled out of the classroom, and about ten minutes later, two male students came to the locked door asking for their phones. She shook her head no and motioned for them to go out on the yard. They turned away for another five minutes, and soon, they and nearly all the students were outside of the door, some of them crying to please give them their phones.

It is obviously time to take a vacation from social media and begin to learn about ourselves and pay attention to our words and sentences.

Our words are powerful!

Because our words are potent, we need to speak only of what is favorable for us and others.

21

It is crucial to take full responsibility for the sentences that come out of our mouths, words written by our hands, or transmitted in any way.

It is imperative that we do not just make noise to fill the silence. What is said stays in the mind and heart of the person or audience we are addressing.

Know that our reality is being created by what we say and do!

Before communicating, ask: Is what I am about to say true? Is it necessary? Is it kind? If what you are about to communicate is not all three, stop! Speak only of what is best for you, all other people, and the world!

Therefore, always remember this simple phrase:

*When I am about to communicate
in my thinking, writing, speaking, or video,
stop and ask:*

*Is it true?
Is it necessary?
Is it kind?
If not all three, do not communicate!*

Chapter 6

Reviewing Your Life

Who are you in the midst of change?

In this time of isolation and retreat, you may want to spend some time journaling. Keep a written record of your actions, thoughts and feelings. If you are struggling with stress, depression, or anxiety, it makes sense to keep a journal to help create a meaningful connection with yourself.

When you write down what is happening in your life and how you feel about it, you gain better control of your emotions and improve your mental health and memory.

This daily exercise of noting what you are doing and thinking can help prioritize problems and fears. You get a clearer picture of what triggers negative thoughts and behaviors and how to solve problems more effectively.

Look at your memories and review and reflect upon successes and failures. It is important to be fair to yourself and strive for balance. Remember, everyone makes mistakes and has reason to regret words spoken and actions taken. That is the past. Forgive yourself and others and let it go.

Project into the future and discover what kind of life might be truly meaningful to you. Direct your thinking toward enhancing your strength, resilience, flexibility, and fortitude. Begin to activate your creativity and ingenuity and be ready to receive new ideas and opportunities. Open your heart to feelings of optimism and empowerment.

A vital ingredient of a successful life is balance, which can stabilize the contrast between the left brain: logic and common sense, and the right brain: creativity and intuition.

But what happens if you feel conflicted, and you hear voices arguing inside your head?

Chapter 7

Emotionally Fractured

How to win the battle inside of you.

M any people complain that they experience voices telling them what to do in their heads. It seems as if parts
of them are trying to get their attention. I am *not* referring to
people who are diagnosed with schizophrenia or are suffering
from multiple personality disorder. People who feel divided
can be average individuals who are busy in the world. When I
mention the word "fractured" or "fragmented," they reply,
"That's me! My mind is never quiet!"

When we are in a *fractured* state, it is difficult to manifest
what we desire. When we are caught in a merry-go-round of
confusing messages, conflicting emotions, and desires, we
may not realize that there is another way of living in the world.

We like to think we are *Captain of our Ship* and *Master of
our Fate.* But I believe we are *Captain of a Pirate Ship, and
the crew is planning mutiny.*

Onboard the ship, the arguments continue, "I want to go
to work!" "No, I want to go to the beach!" And another says,
"I want to go home!" As the arguments continue, we wonder
which way is the right way to go.

It is common to experience internal confusion when the world is changing so quickly. We may feel like Humpty Dumpty who fell off a wall and broke into a thousand pieces!

The feeling of being *emotionally fractured* is when thousands of opposing beliefs, thoughts, and feelings move through the mind and bump into each other.

Where do all these beliefs originate?

Most people absorb various conflicting beliefs from their families, friends, teachers, advertising, and the media. These subconscious concepts about yourself, other people, society, the government, and the world often trigger emotions, which may erupt without warning or understanding.

> *The mind compartmentalizes and assigns each belief to a subpersonality who attempts to prove it's true.*

The subpersonality's job is to guard, protect, and continuously prove a belief by accumulating information that verifies its truth. Another subpersonality holds an opposing belief, and then the battle begins. An example:

Belief: "It would be great to be rich!"
Opposing belief: "Being rich means paying high taxes. People might like you only for your money, etc."
Belief: "Being healthy is important."

Opposing belief: "There are advantages of being sick, like resting, getting away from work, getting attention, etc."

Belief: "A loving relationship would add to my life."
Opposing belief: "It is better to be free. I don't have to answer to anyone else."

As you might know, it is challenging to clear your mind and listen to your heart when you are arguing with yourself.

When we are emotionally fractured,
we are fighting with ourselves.

Each sub-personality within us insists that their ideas are correct. Even though some of their concepts stop us from achieving our goals, these representatives of opposing beliefs **always think they are helping us.**

But it doesn't make "sense" that a sub-personality
thinks it is helping us by stopping progress!

What are the advantages of...
- *Feeling sick and tired?*
- *Having barely enough money?*
- *Being alone? (Not in relationship)*
- *Bored and creatively unfulfilled?*

After counseling several thousand people, I know *for sure* that there are subpersonalities (parts of us) who have positive reasons for blocking what we desire in our lives. *That part of us thinks they are doing something FOR us.*

So how can we get to neutral? Is there a way to establish a consensus of these fractured parts so that the subpersonalities unite and work together to create our hearts' desires?

Yes, it is possible to bring the fractured parts of us together. We can combine the positive aspects of the opposing beliefs to end the argument and regain our power.

First, we need to discover the beliefs that are stopping us and what their point of view is doing FOR us.

Some beliefs may be helpful during certain periods in our lives to help us grow, learn lessons, and become more aware. Eventually, when we receive more evidence to the contrary, those beliefs may no longer enable us to develop into who we can be.

A simple combination of words can become a belief. When an authoritative person repeats a statement several times, it will likely stay in our minds and become a belief. The same phrase is often used repeatedly by different media to make a point appear to be true.

An example: Whenever it rained, my Mom would say, "Cover your head. Don't get wet. You will catch a cold." Without fail, covered or not, I would start sneezing after being out in the rain.

A teacher might warn a student, "You don't have the talent or mental ability to be a _____. (Name the activity or profession. It could be a doctor, lawyer, scientist, economist, artist, actor, computer programmer, designer, etc.)

If that negative statement of "not being capable" sticks in their mind and becomes a belief, the person may not even try.

Look around you. Think about those people who go beyond expectations and become wildly successful!

What made the difference? *Those who go forward and challenge the odds don't turn negative statements into beliefs.* They are aware that each person has a world view about themselves and others. Successful people don't believe in the failure point of view. And even if they fail, they start again and look at failure as an essential step toward their success.

When listening to others, no matter who they might be, take a moment to ask, "Is that statement an opinion or a fact." Facts can be distorted and are actually opinions. In the news, what we hear should be "taken with a grain of salt."

What does that mean, "Take it with a grain of salt?" That phrase became popular in the 17th Century and meant that since food tastes better with a grain of salt, listening to out-landish or barely true stories also should be accompanied adding salt.

The tabloids and gossip magazines often invent
stories about celebrities, so you should
take what you read with a grain of salt.

The point is, listen closely to the meaning of what people say. Shift negative statements into positive affirmations. Discover what makes you happy, and be grateful for what you have. Lift your thoughts to form a brighter future.

We will explore the Infusion Integration Technique and how it unites your opposing subpersonalities in Chapter 18.

But first, who is to blame for the problems in your life?

Chapter 8

Reflection/Deflection

Who is to Blame?

One of the favorite ways to handle the problems and difficulties in our lives is to blame others. There is no lack of those to blame. Parents and other relatives provide handy whipping posts, and there are teachers, bosses, personal relationships, friends, people in authority, etc.

Excuses for anger and frustration often result in statements like, *that person said or did this or that*, which *made me do that or this!*

So who is to blame? Or should we blame anyone?

In my many years of studying human behavior and emotional healing, I have learned that most of us don't understand how connected we are to each other. What we think and feel act as magnets attracting people who think and feel the same way.

*You magnetize matching frequencies of beliefs.
"Birds of a feather flock together."*

The people and environment around you may displease certain parts-of-you, but who you are with and where you live are probably "normal" for you because you have experienced it in childhood and perhaps numerous times since. Where you are in your life and who you are with typically matches what you think is "reality." Your current life may not fit your desires, but it does represent your beliefs.

Other people mirror the beliefs
and concepts you hold within you.

Here are some questions you might ask:

- Are you surrounded by loving, supportive people?
- Do the people you care about approve of your behavior, i.e. how you look and what you do in your life?
- Do you feel valued and appreciated?
- Are you well and happy?
- Does your life run smoothly with high points that make you feel more vibrant and alive?

If not, why not?

Chapter 9

Your Life Is a Bio-Feedback System

Does your life show you what you believe?

If we think about the amount of programming we received over the years, is it any wonder that other people's ideas, concepts, and beliefs have become rooted in our minds?

All the positive and negative phrases keep repeating in our subconscious and are in the background unsettling our emotions and blocking our progress as we try to do our best.

Friends who are close to us and even strangers will say or act out what we think, feel, and believe. Statements are made to us that we either like or hate, reflecting what we hold in our minds' inner landscape.

The idea that people are reflecting
our thoughts is very unnerving.

If we pay close attention, we may notice that some of the negative statements spoken to us are the very thoughts we fight against in our minds. Complimentary words are often positive thoughts we were thinking about ourselves. Life is a bio-feedback system, and what we are thinking and feeling shows up outside of us.

It is incredible, but often a person will say **the exact words** you have been thinking. Arguments begin when someone says the same bad thought you said to yourself.

Examples of negative inner thoughts we reflect to another person who speaks that thought to us.

∞   ∞   ∞

Your mother or close friend says, "Oh, it looks like that outfit is a little tight on you. Have you gained weight?"
You answer: *"No, it was always tight. You are always finding fault with me. Leave me alone!"*
(**Hidden thought:** I raid the refrigerator late at night, and I've gained weight.)

∞   ∞   ∞

Another Example:
Partner: "You're lying. Why aren't you telling the truth?"
You answer: *"I never lie to you. You are the liar!"*
(**Hidden Thought:** I can't tell them the truth about that.)

∞   ∞   ∞

Boss: "You're late every day. Don't you like your job?"
You answer: *"Oh, of course, I like my job. You know how the traffic is."*
(**Hidden thought:** I don't like this job, and I wish they'd fire me so I could get unemployment.")

∞   ∞   ∞

Partner: "This place is a mess. You sure don't like to clean, do you?"

You: *"Listen to me...Why don't you take care of the kids, the dog, the food, the bills, and see if you want to clean house!"*

(**Hidden thought**: I hate cleaning the house.)

∞　　∞　　∞

Pleasant examples of positive inner thoughts about you reflecting for another person to say.

♥　♥　♥

Friend: "You look wonderful today. Did you get a new hairstyle?"

You: *"Thank you so much. Yes, I did change my hair."*

(**Hidden thought:** I really like this new hairstyle. I think it makes me look good.)

♥　♥　♥

Associate: "You're doing a great job on that project. I think you deserve a raise."

You: *"Thank you. I really appreciate the opportunity."*

(**Hidden thought:** I enjoy this project. If I do a great job, maybe I'll get a raise.)

♥　♥　♥

Friend: "You have great ideas. You should seek a community leadership position."

You: *"Thank you. I love helping people."*

(**Hidden thought:** I would like to be in a position that I can help the community more effectively.)

Our environment is continuously and consistently feeding back to us what we are thinking and feeling. So how do we respond when someone says what we don't want to hear?

If we dare, the best idea is to answer with the truth, starting with the simple statement, "Yes, you are right."

I know it isn't easy to acknowledge what we were trying to hide, but unfortunately, we cannot hide anything in this time of rapid change.

All the blinders are coming off.
The secrets are coming out of the closet
and out from under the bed.
Nothing can be hidden.

Think deeply about life being a bio-feedback system and ask yourself these questions:

- If my thoughts and beliefs create my reality, what was I thinking to bring forth the problems, arguments, blockages, anxiety, accidents, and confusion in my life?

Often we are thinking about what is wrong with our life. We worry about what will happen next? Will we be able to handle the problems as they arise, such as:

Negative: What if I get sick? What if there is an accident?
Positive: I am well. When I drive I am always safe.

Negative: What if the car won't start or I have a flat tire?
Positive: I checked the car, and it is in good shape.

Negative: I don't like what that person did, and I am going to give them a piece of my mind? (An interesting phrase we use when we have an argument.)
Positive: I'll let that go. There's no need to get angry.

Negative: I can't get ahead financially. I'm going broke.
Positive: My finances are getting better and better.

- What beliefs and hidden concepts are floating in the back of my mind that make me feel uncomfortable, unlovable, unhealthy, unlucky, and out-of-control?

Uncomfortable Belief: I always feel awkward.
Comfortable: I can relax and feel self-assured.

Unlovable Belief: No one cares about me.

Lovable: I love myself and other people.

Unhealthy: I can easily catch a disease.
Healthy: I feel great and my immune system is fine.

Unlucky: I have the worst luck and can't win!
Lucky: I'm the luckiest person in the world!

Out of Control: I'm going crazy every day!
In Control: I can handle anything that comes my way!

Continue looking at your environment and the people around you to learn more about what you are thinking. **When you change your thoughts, statements, and beliefs, which are the seeds of your reality, you change your life.**

Chapter 10

From Fractured to Neutral

How do you find your center?

Each of us has a center point, a place where our mind and Spirit meet, bringing us to a higher level of awareness, harmony, and peace. Look in the mirror and note that your physical center is at your belly button. Therefore, in the Eastern tradition, the meditator concentrates on their belly.

The heart is the center of emotions and works with the brain to think. When speaking of the mind, the Buddhists always point to their heart, where mindfulness originates.

By diffusing the emotions attached to beliefs, you allow your mind to rest in a state of neutrality, regaining your judgement, conscience, and rationality. You begin to feel at ease and at peace, thus shifting and improving your experiences. You find yourself making new connections and discovering unexpected pathways to success.

This movement into neutrality begins by selecting an area in your life that you would like to change. The primary areas of our life are health, wealth, relationships, and creativity. I call these the *Four Cornerstones of Life*. If any of these cornerstones are missing, the building (our life) begins to tilt.

Since we are dealing with emotions, let us consider the wide variety of negative emotions that arise in response to upsetting people and events.

The Negative Emotions of FEAR Include:	
Outer	**Inner**
Annoyance	Anxiety
Disgust	Worry
Frustration	Guilt
Hate	Shame
Anger	Jealousy
Rage	Panic
Disappointment	
Loneliness & Sadness	
Hopelessness	
Depression & Despair	

Anger and all other negative emotions are each a part of fear. The opposite of fear is Love, which is joyful, hopeful, warm, and comforting. Love is calm, relaxed, patient, and at peace.

What Causes Fear?

Fear is activated by external stressors that appear to be a threat to our health and well-being. Fear is always about the future. We fear what is going to happen next, in a few minutes, hours, days, weeks, months, or years from now. Our ultimate fear is the unknown, especially death. Yet, over 75% of us and more than 90% for some religious people, believe in life after death.

Still, we spend a lot of time needlessly worrying to the point of mental or physical disease. Stress often causes internal anxiety that can lead to behaviors or addictions that can further fracture us and create severe problems in our lives.

The Opposite of Fear is LOVE

Love is all the positive emotions. Loving is happiness, excited, delighted, caring, joyful, hopeful, warm, and comforting. It is calm, relaxed, patient, and at peace. Love is contentment, serenity, awe, interest, hope, amusement, and inspiration.

Excerpt from *A Course in Miracles*:

There Are No Idle Thoughts

"Everyone experiences fear. Yet, it would take very little right thinking to realize why fear occurs. Few appreciate the real power of the mind, and no one remains fully aware of it all the time.

"However, if you hope to spare yourself from fear there are some things you must realize, and realize fully. The mind is very powerful, and never loses its creative force. It never sleeps. Every instant it is creating. It is hard to recognize that thought and belief combine into a power surge that can literally move mountains.

"It appears at first glance that to believe such power about yourself is arrogant, but that is not the real reason you do not believe it. You prefer to believe that your thoughts cannot exert real influence because you are actually afraid of them.

"This may allay awareness of the guilt, but at the cost of perceiving the mind as impotent. If you believe that what you think is ineffectual you may cease to be afraid of it, but you are hardly likely to respect it.

"There *are* no idle thoughts. All thinking produces form at some level."　　　　– A Course in Miracles
Chapter 2 – VI. Fear and Conflict

We have the power to control and stand guard over our thoughts. It is possible for each of us to make the decision not to pursue whatever subject is nagging us. We can choose not go down into a rabbit-hole of negativity.

Turn your attention to something beautiful, uplifting, and encouraging. Laugh out loud to wake up and break the spell of a past drama replaying in your mind.

You are far more powerful than you have ever imagined!

Chapter 11

What about Obsessive Behavior?

Are we caught in compulsive actions?

Thinking worrisome and fearful thoughts may lead to uncontrollable behavior and addictions. The anxiety we are holding can become Obsessive-Compulsive Behavior when images and impulses keep repeating like a needle stuck in an old record. This behavior may interfere with our daily lives and can lead to using alcohol and drugs as self-medication.

There are ways in which we can handle stress whether or not we are diagnosed with O.C.D. Some of us may feel compelled to act out these behaviors occasionally in our lives.

People with Obsessive-Compulsive Behavior fall into the following categories described by HelpGuide.org:

- **Washers** are afraid of contamination and have cleaning or hand-washing compulsions.
- **Checkers** repeatedly check things (oven off, door locked, etc.) that may cause harm or danger.
- **Doubters and sinners** think everything needs to be perfect or done just right.
- **Counters and arrangers** are obsessed with order and symmetry, and maybe superstitious about numbers, colors, or arrangements.

- **Hoarders** are afraid to throw things away and compulsively hoard things not needed or used.

Self-help tips for O.C.D. include:
- Identify the thoughts that bring on the compulsions.
- Face the triggers and learn to resist urges to complete compulsive rituals.
- Challenge obsessive thoughts by writing them down and ask: Is this idea helpful?
  - What's the evidence that the fear is real?
  - What's the probability that it will happen?
  - Is there a more positive way to view the situation?
  - What would I say to a friend who had this thought?
  - Reach out to family, friends, or a support group.

Ways to handle stress:
- Do physical exercise. Take a walk each day.
- Connect with another person face-to-face.
- Use your senses - listen to music, look at a pleasant scene, savor a cup of tea, or stroke a pet.
- Practice relaxation techniques - yoga, deep breathing, and other ways to rest and distract the mind.

Chapter 12

Releasing Addictions

*Drug, alcohol, and food cravings
throw us off balance.*

As you know, thoughts and beliefs have been ingrained in our psyche and are difficult to change. One of the most challenging habits to release is an addiction, which threatens our stability and emotional balance.

The most important factors that make quitting an addiction difficult are *tolerance* **and** *withdrawal.* They are intertwined and are primary reasons a person becomes addicted.

The first time we encounter an addictive substance may be overwhelming or unpleasant, or it can be mild and pleasurable. The more we use drugs or alcohol, the less sensitive we are, and specific parts of the brain are affected, creating physical *tolerance.* Behaviors such as sex and gambling produce feelings of excitement that get less intense over time. *We need more to feel the same effect.*

When we try to stop, we experience physical and psychological *withdrawal symptoms*: shaking, stomach upsets, and feeling anxious and depressed. The one thing you depended on to cope with stress has now become off-limits.

Food addiction is just like drug and alcohol addiction!

When we eat addictive foods, the brain's **"reward circuit"** lights up and is flooded with the chemical messenger dopamine. We can become addicted to foods that are high in sugar, flour, fat, grains, and salt, or some combination of these.

We seek the foods we crave. We often eat more of these addictive foods to achieve the previous high, making us think we feel so much better. We find ourselves rummaging through the cupboard and refrigerator, looking for our favorite treats.

We often cannot control the urge to eat unhealthy food, which makes us overweight and susceptible to diabetes and heart disease. It is best to keep addictive food out of the house.

What if there were a way to settle your mind and feel more in control?

How can we shift the stress, anxiety, and fear into a feeling of strength, confidence, and courage? The root of courage is *"cor"* –Latin word for heart. In one of its earliest forms, courage meant *"To speak one's mind by telling all one's heart."*

What does this have to do with moving from *"Fractured"* to *"Neutral?"* It means that rather than arguing with ourselves, we could learn to have the courage to move forward with resolve, sharing our best selves with others.

Chapter 13

Lifting the Cloud of Depression

Never give up hope.

G oing through a Pandemic certainly rates as one of the obvious times in history when becoming depressed would seem to be inevitable. Although everyone may feel the pressure of the Pandemic, some people who have felt depressed in the past may find that this unpredictable, seemingly endless threat is making their depression worse.

There are a variety of concepts of why we fall into depression. As pointed out earlier, we have within us opposing, hidden beliefs that often keep us in emotional turmoil. Depression is repressed anger, and it happens when we do not or cannot express those emotions outwardly. Instead, we turn negative thoughts and feelings inward and attack ourselves.

Some of these beliefs include:
1. I am all alone. No one cares for me.
2. The world is falling apart, and so am I.
3. I don't have enough money, time, or energy.
4. There is no future for me.
5. I don't fit in. I am ugly, awkward, stupid, a misfit.

All of these beliefs revolve around a central theme: Your self-image and what you think other people think about you.

There is an interesting story about a renowned reconstructive surgeon, Maxwell Maltz, M.D., who created Psycho-Cybernetics, which means *steering your mind to a productive and useful goal so you can reach the greatest port in the world: your peace of mind.*

In the 1920s, Dr. Maltz was among the first to perfect reconstructive surgical techniques. Educated at Columbia, he began treating patients, including victims of burns and accidents, those who suffered deformities or congenital disabilities, which impaired their daily functioning.

After years of medical practice, Dr. Maltz made a startling observation: Most of his patients *experienced* a marked improvement in self-image following successful surgeries; yet, for some people, their self-image stayed the same. He wondered why they didn't see themselves differently.

Maltz became convinced that self-image is mostly the result of self-perceptions and unconscious messages. These ideas are internalized and keep repeating from an early age. Negative concepts can be crippling, and it is possible to change those beliefs.

The simplest way to change self-image beliefs is to catch the negative, insulting sentences that degrade, dehumanize, and dishonor you. Taking the earlier statements, change the negative to positive: Negative words have a negative charge. Making positive comments reinforces and strengthens you.

- I am all alone. No one cares for me.
Change to: I am All One, whole, and complete. I am a Being of Love and Light, and everyone loves me.

- The world is falling apart, and so am I.
Change to: The world is self-sufficient, and I am well and safe from harm.

- I don't have enough money, time, or vitality.
Change to: I receive more than enough money and have plenty of time and vitality.

- There is no future for me.
Change to: I am ready to meet the future with vitality and strength. Opportunities are available to me.

- I don't fit in. I am ugly, awkward, stupid, a misfit.
Change to: I am a beautiful Being of Light, graceful, intelligent, and an example of joy and peace.

How can we help ourselves overcome depression? First of all, be aware that depression is common. Millions of people are facing similar challenges, emotions, and obstacles.

Here are some ideas to help yourself out of depression:

- **It is crucial that you accept and love yourself as you are.** Imagine hugging your inner child and you.
- **Learn the sound of your "depression voice"** and do the opposite of what it is saying. Use logic as your weapon, and answer each thought as it comes to mind.
- **Write down the good things that happen during the day and then note what went wrong.** Discover what makes your mood, emotions, and thoughts change. Forgive the feelings and opinions of the day. Set up micro-goals as you look forward to starting again tomorrow.
- **Develop a gentle, new routine.** As you practice setting up time periods, you may feel more connected, and the tasks can help organize your mind.
- **Do something you enjoy to break the patterns of thought that are stuck in your mind.** Listen to music, dance to the beat, go out in nature, take a walk, do a puzzle, spend time with other people.
- **Look into vitamin supplements,** such as Omega-3 found in fatty fish, Vitamins B from eggs, dairy, meat and fish, D from the sun, Turmeric, and Probiotics, etc.

Can we lift the cloud of depression? YES! When we commit to feeling happier and more alive, our decision helps us find what we are seeking. Dealing with depression or other diseases requires a willingness to try many possible solutions. Certainly, self-help techniques and shifting beliefs can help.

Yet, if we experience prolonged depression, it is best to make an appointment with your doctor and follow their instructions and advice. Severe depression symptoms can include the inability to experience pleasure, no enthusiasm, difficulty concentrating, trouble sleeping or eating, and the feeling of being disconnected from life.

People struggling with depression can experience fulfilling lives if they seek treatment to help manage their condition. Several forms of psychotherapy and anti-depressants treat depression, and receiving effective treatment reduces the time spent suffering and feeling dysfunctional.

In the process of healing from depression, it is also helpful to look beyond this earthly plane and expand your view of life and its meaning.

Open your mind and heart to a belief in a power greater than yourself. Such an idea can help you maintain hope as you move forward with determination and the assistance you need to achieve your goal.

When we view ourselves as on a spiritual path, our problems no longer appear as obstacles. Instead, we see each challenge as an opportunity for growth and learning.

Creating a spiritual connection to whatever name you call God or the Angels can make all the difference in your life. It is not required to follow any dogma; you simply need to know in your heart that you are far more than your body, mind, and emotions.

There are certainly good reasons to lift the cloud of depression, such as enjoying family, friends, and the beauty of this Earth. You are a spiritual being who transcends the physical and will be regenerated by the feeling of Universal Love.

In Larry Dossey's book, *Prayer Is Good Medicine*, he reports the following:

"More than 130 controlled laboratory studies show, in general, that prayer or prayer-like states of compassion, empathy, and love can bring helpful changes in many types of living things, from humans to bacteria. This does not mean prayer always works, any more than drugs or surgery always works, but that, statistically speaking, prayer is effective."

So, what if you could lessen the underlying emotions of anxiety and fear and replace them with calm and peace?

Chapter 14

Listen to Your Heart

What is heart intelligence?

Your real power is the ability to make choices and take actions that serve yourself and empower others.
The title of the first metaphysical book I read, "As a Man Thinketh" by James Allen, is based on Proverbs 23:7: *"For as a Man Thinketh in his Heart, so is he."* I find it interesting that this Proverb mentions *"Thinketh in his Heart."*

In the past thirty years, there has been much progress in regards to understanding the heart-mind connection. I have been acquainted with Greg Braden and *HeartMath Institute*. They have been studying heart intelligence and have found:

"Heart intelligence is the flow of awareness, under-standing, and intuition we experience when the mind and emotions are brought into coherent alignment with the heart. Pioneer neuro-cardiologist at Heart-Math, Andrew Armour, introduced the term "heart brain." He said the heart possessed a complex and in-trinsic nervous system that is a brain."

HeartMath Institute has also found that "The heart is the most powerful source of electromagnetic energy in the human body, producing the largest rhythmic electromagnetic field of any of the body's organs. The heart's electrical field is about 60 times greater in amplitude than electrical activity generated by the brain.

HeartMath has found that the heart is in a constant two-way dialog with the brain. We now know that emotions have as much to do with the heart and body as they do with the brain. Of the bodily organs, the heart plays a particularly important role in our emotional experience with the heart, brain, and body acting in concert.

When we experience uplifting emotions such as appreciation, joy, care, and love; our heart rhythm pattern becomes highly ordered, looking like a smooth, harmonious wave.
(There are excellent books and videos by Greg Braden available at www.HeartMath.com.)

You have the power of heart, mind, and soul to direct your life in a positive direction. The higher emotional frequency can help you experience a greater awareness with expanded creativity, capability, resourcefulness, and achievement.

As you clear away the past, you will gain perspective and open to new visions for the future. Using your intuition to connect you to Guidance, you can focus on ingenuity, inventiveness, inspiration, and imagination to improve your life and gain the confidence to fulfill your purpose and fondest dreams.

The baggage of the past is almost always about loss. And we don't like losing. Battles, arguments, and confusion cause pain, and our minds lose control.

We don't like feeling lost in our loss.

Therefore, it is essential to your well-being to release emotional patterns that wear on your nerves, and, like background noise, the thoughts and emotions continue to add to your stress levels. Those negative events that haunt you often repeat and show up again and again in your future.

Why? Because when you keep going over upsetting past people and events in your mind, you maintain the matching frequency of those people and events. That energetic frequency magnetizes the same negativity to you over and over again. Similar problems, confusion, difficulties with relationships, lack of finances, and unpleasant workplaces, etc. show up in your life. The same people with the same attitudes keep reappearing, with different faces and names.

Isn't it time to release the old programming and allow new people, events, and environments to enter your life? Create a unique view of the world, raise your liveliness to a new frequency, and your future will begin changing from negative to positive today.

"The progressive nature of our existence constantly moves us forward, and in its wake, we must let go of the past or become lost in its future.

"Sometimes what we think we want is irrelevant to what we need. Regardless of our willingness to accept, understand, or prepare for our conditions, we still move forward. *Time is the master by which all things must pass.*"

– Ranse Parker, *Circle of Doors, Chapter: Mirrors*

Chapter 15

Learning from Relationships

What was the Gift?

There are times when a particular statement stays in our minds and hearts. One of those times was when I was listening to a CD by Carolyn Myss, best-selling author and medical intuitive. She was talking about *finding the gift* in every experience, and she asked the question, *"What did you learn in an event or a relationship that you can take with you and apply to the future?"*

We each have confusing experiences, especially in the realm of relationships. It is fascinating to see how the dynamics between people can change. Whether it is a family member, a friend or acquaintance, a person we are dating, someone we are living with, or a marriage partner, our interactions can grow in caring and love, or become antagonistic and fade away.

What is the gift in a relationship? The gift, at its best, is that we experience loving friendship and support. The other person becomes our mirror, helping us to learn more about ourselves: what we care about, our thoughts and beliefs, talents and abilities, and our levels of tolerance and patience.

Personal relationships can be enriching, yet we are often upset with the very people we have chosen to be in our lives. We feel that they don't understand us, nor do they provide the loving behavior we crave. They are elsewhere in mind and spirit. Together, we may drift through our lives, sharing space, paying bills, and raising children, while wondering who we are living with after all.

How can relationships be changed for the better?

Relationships change when we release negative beliefs and replace them with positive thoughts about what might be possible. We will find ourselves acting differently. When we visualize a life filled with love, good humor, financial security, good health, and joyful experiences, the process of creating that scenario begins. *Every change in our lives starts with our state of mind.*

It is helpful to take the time to imagine being able to communicate easily at a deeper level about who you are and what you would like your life to be. Find out about the people in your life. What do they think and feel? Which activities do they enjoy? Visualize growing closer together, expanding your mutual interests, and falling deeper in love each day.

If you don't have a close relationship, choose wisely.

Take time to get to know the person you are dating. Learn about all aspects of his or her past and present from his friends and family. Too few people *due diligence,* as is practiced in the financial world when people set up a business relationship.

What does *due diligence* mean? It means we investigate the person we have chosen and confirm the facts about their life, including their finances. *Trust is of the utmost importance in any partnership.* Living together and getting married is always a business arrangement, as well as a love affair.

Always listen to your intuition!

We often do not pay attention to the little and sometimes big red flags on the field when interacting with others. People always give us cues to their true nature and their intentions. When we meet in-person, we can read body language, but we must carefully examine the writing in an email or text message. What are they saying? Often, we fool ourselves and don't want to acknowledge what we have seen, heard, or felt.

We mustn't feel in *desperate need* of a relationship, especially when meeting unknown men and women on the internet. You can't be too aware and cautious in giving out your information or falling for a lie. There are expensive scams in social media, and it's not worth the heartache to learn the truth too late.

How can you find true love?

Think for a moment about the feeling of being in love. Sit back and sense the excitement and the overflowing feeling of joy.

When you are in love, everything seems to sparkle, and you feel buoyant as if you can float on air.

Indeed, Love is so much more than caring about another person. The power of Love is in the very air that you breathe and the beat of your heart. The Universal flow of life moving through you and out into the world is Love.

I remember a special moment when I was in the delightful feeling of being in love. I happened to be in Rome, and as I stood in awe looking at the magnificent Trevi Fountain, a thought entered my mind, *What if I could always feel this way? What if the feeling of Love didn't depend on another person? What if I could fall in love with life?* I decided to make a life-long commitment of being in love with life!

You can fall in love with life and also be in love with YOU, unconditionally. No matter your faults and weaknesses, it is time to begin a *Lifelong Love Affair with YOU.* Become your new best friend, and love yourself with all your heart and soul. Be honest, trustworthy, kind, and caring to yourself for the rest of your life. That deep, abiding Love will overflow to others, and you will create an environment of harmony, joy, and peace.

Chapter 16

How Do You Forgive?

What is the procedure for forgiveness?

Forgiveness is the key to health and well-being. *For-giving* means *giving forward*. In other words, we give ourselves a more positive future by forgiving and letting go of the past. We don't have to *forget* what happened, but we can release the emotional charge, which is blocked energy, imprisoning us in a constant spiral of unhealthy thoughts.

After an upsetting or fearful event, psychologists, religious leaders, and friends almost always mention that it is best to forgive what has happened to us. The hurtful person may be a family member, a loved one, a teacher, co-worker or boss, a friend or enemy, an acquaintance, stranger, politician, or yourself. The process of forgiveness helps us release the pain.

How to Forgive? We can forgive whatever upsets us, whether it is personal or for other people, when it happens or days, months, or years later. It often helps to write about our experience and why it is hurtful. Journaling can give us an objective view and start to clear our minds, hearts, and emotions.

If we consider the idea that what we experience is a projection of our own subconscious into the dream-like world around us, then we are indeed forgiving ourselves for unknowingly participating in creating the dream. Forgiveness is releasing the underlying fear and pain we have carried within us.

We may never understand why the event happened, but forgiving the person or experience can set us free, and the memory will begin to fade away.

We will feel lighter and more available to live our lives. We can rest in knowing that our forgiveness opens the door to meet new friends, develop new opportunities, and to learn once again to enjoy life to the fullest.

The following poem seems appropriate.

The way it was…
The way it is…
The way it wants to be
is the way you'll always see.

The why it is, is the way you are.
The why is neither near nor far…
the why is moving round and round
inside you…waiting to be found!

--John Teressi, *"Portals in Time:*
The Quest for Un-Old Age"

Chapter 17

Losing a Loved One

How do you handle grief?

Many of us have lost someone close to us, and we know that nothing can prepare us for the emotions of sadness and pain that follow the death of a person we love.

It is helpful to find sanctuary in religious and spiritual beliefs that death is indeed a transition to another dimension where the soul continues. In that state of being, our loved one can send us love and guidance as we continue to live in physical form.

The belief about life after death has been given credence by people who have had near-death and out-of-body experiences. Those who have traveled beyond the veil all say that after leaving their body, they see a tunnel, which leads to a bright light opening to a new vista. Friends or relatives who have passed away are there to greet them. Some see brilliant, natural settings and cities of light. They feel intense love that fills their heart and soul.

At various times after our loved one has transitioned, we may experience the sense that they are still with us. We might hear a message in our minds or see them in our dreams. These visitations can feel like communication from them, and it also is a way for our minds to reconcile and heal the loss.

Whether or not we believe in life after death, *we need to regain our balance* when someone we care for passes away. It is crucial to take care of our body by paying attention to food, exercise, and sleep. We need to love ourselves during these difficult times since stress can take a toll on our bodies.

Accepting support from family, friends, a community or church grief support group, or seeing a professional counselor can help us go through the grieving process.

When the grief seems overwhelming, it is often surprising to look back at your life and realize that you have not taken the time to acknowledge the large and small losses you have experienced. The feeling of loss may have piled up, and now is the moment you truly need to forgive those experiences and let them go.

Know you can and will move forward, holding the memory of that person and what they meant to you close to your heart.

When someone you love is a memory,
their memory becomes a treasure.

Chapter 18

Infusion Integration Technique

Can you bring together parts-of-you
with opposing beliefs?

The *Infusion Integration Technique* helps to bring together the parts-of-us who hold opposing beliefs. We can heal the feeling of being "fractured," become whole, regain our full power and sense of well-being.

Integrating conflicting parts of us can help create balance and inner peace. We can help them change behavior by integrating opposing beliefs. The word *Infusion* means the moment that Spirit enters form. Thus, when we combine parts of us who are opposed, we allow the higher aspect of ourselves to heal our division.

The following is an abbreviated version of the *Infusion Integration Technique* (I.I.T), which I explain in more detail in my books "Ending the Battle Within" and "The Heart of Transformation and the Butterfly Effect." I have used this process for over thirty years, and it has been highly useful to release stress and fear for me and others.

I have read that some scientists think that the mind holds beliefs and memories in a crystalline form. If that concept is correct, when you integrate opposing beliefs, you are melting the crystals. The two opposing patterns of beliefs unite and work together in a way that serves the body, mind, and emotions, helping you shift direction in your life. When doing the process, it actually feels like that is happening in your head.

The *Infusion Integration Technique* **is similar to two people going to a counselor to work out their differences**. Each person explains the positive reasons for what they are doing or saying. The Observer listens and then works with them to find common ground to eliminate disagreements and confusion. In this example, we will focus on integrating the emotion of fear with the feeling of peace.

One of the subpersonalities will be called *Fearful.* The other will be *Peaceful, and e*ach hand will represent one of these parts of you.

You are the *Observer* or *Counselor* who is neutral. The following is an example of a dialog for the *Infusion Integration Technique* to calm your fears and become peaceful.

Your responses must always be positive. A negative answer to why you don't want to be successful would be: "I am afraid of success." A positive answer is: "I would rather not be successful because I enjoy privacy and being anonymous."

The question is: What are the opposing parts of you doing FOR you? This process is being presented in the first person for you to imagine yourself doing the integration technique.

As Observer, you ask: I would like to ask either my left or right hand to represents anxiety and fear. As an example, you choose the right hand.

Observer: Hello. I will call you *Fearful*. I would like to ask, "What are you doing FOR me?"

Imagine that you are assuming *Fearful's* point of view, the part-of-you who keeps you in fear. Wave the right hand that Fearful occupies to show that it is going to speak.

Fearful speaks: What I am doing FOR you? I keep you anxious and afraid to keep you on guard at all times to stay safe. You have to be aware and alert!

It's a scary world (underlying belief), and you have to pay attention to what is happening around you, on the news, and what could happen tomorrow. Look, there are fires, storms, Covid-19 is still spreading, and you could fall and hurt yourself. Or someone could attack you. You need more money, food might get scarce, and the list goes on and on. Plus, sometimes, you have to get angry and yell at upsetting experiences to release all that pent-up power.

Observer: Thank you for sharing. That's quite a long list!

Fearful: I could think of a lot more things for you to fear!

Observer: Yes, I understand that you could always add to the list. But let me turn to the other hand now.

I would like to talk to the part of me representing calm and peace on my left hand. *Peaceful,* what are you doing FOR me?

Peaceful: I am trying to provide a safe harbor where you can calm down and relax. I encourage you to breathe fully and connect with your heart to feel love you need to sustain your health and well-being. I try to connect you to your higher self and encourage listening to your intuition, which will always guide you correctly if you pay attention and follow the guidance. You need to be calm in the midst of confusion and chaos.

Observer: Thank you, *Peaceful,* for the work you are doing. You have helped me to calm down and stay sane when I have felt afraid and angry.

I would now like to talk to my *Fearful* representative again and ask you: What if you could keep my safe, and I didn't have to be anxious and afraid a great deal of the time.

Fearful: You mean there is a way that you can be safe without feeling anxious and afraid?

Observer: Yes, that is possible if you are willing to change your behavior.

Fearful: I might be open to that idea. What do you propose?

Observer: What if you could feel safe, and the world did not seem so scary, but at the same time, you would be able to protect me, AND I could feel peaceful, listen to my heart, and follow my intuitive guidance. You would let me calm down and relax and not feel so angry, AND I would still be aware of my surroundings and vigilant in my desire to be safe.

Fearful: Well, that would be pretty good if it could happen.

Observer: Thank you for cooperating, *Fearful.*
Now, I would like you to go to the creative part of my being, which you can imagine to be a beautiful room full of magical computers, which contain all information. There are also grand Angels who have Universal knowledge.

You are asking for *three ways* that you can feel safe, secure, and peaceful amid this turmoil, and you don't have to make me feel anxious and afraid with outbursts of anger. If I am in danger, I will remain level-headed and calm enough to move to safety quickly.

You do not need to know what those *three ways* are in consciousness at this time. You will see yourself behaving differently and will no longer need to keep me always alert in fear. Are you willing to allow this change to happen?

Fearful: Yes, as long as you keep safe.

Observer: Good. I would now like all parts-of-my-being to check those *three ways* and ensure that the solutions are a win-win situation for all parts of me.

Now, I hold up my two hands at my chest level with the palms facing each other. The Fearful part-of-me is facing *the Peaceful* part-of-me. They acknowledge each other and realize that both of them had good intentions.

I close my eyes and slowly bring the two palms together until they touch, and the fingers intertwine. Now I see those two parts-of-me hugging each other, and I move my clasped hands up to my heart. I imagine all parts-of-me forming a huddle around these two, sending them love and healing.

I see my higher self, the greater aspect of who I truly am hovering overhead, sending love and healing to all parts of me.

In my imagination, I see Fearful and Peaceful walking hand-in-hand down a pathway rimmed with flowers and up onto a grassy hillside overlooking a stream. The two begin to share concepts and ideas about how they can work together.

Observer: I thank the two of you for sharing your information in consciousness and going through the integration with me. If there are any other parts-of-me that feel as if they are alienated or frustrated, I invite you to speak to me. I will take the time to understand what you are trying to do FOR me and to integrate you into my whole being. And thank you.

Together we can create happiness and peace of mind.

Your sub-conscious will effortlessly work out these solutions without you needing to continue a dialog. In a short period of time, you may see yourself acting in new and different ways that are positive and productive.

Once the conflicting beliefs are resolved, you will experience more passion and may discover new opportunities coming your way.

I have used the Integration Technique for a variety of challenges in my life and others' lives. It is almost miraculous how quickly integration resolves the conflict inside our minds and changes our negative, no longer needed beliefs.

Clearing your opposing beliefs is somewhat similar to *defragmenting* a computer.

Mechanical disks sometimes suffer from a phenomenon called "fragmentation." The more programs and files you use, copy, and move, the more cluttered your disk becomes, and the harder the read/write head has to work to open or store your data.

Does this sound familiar? Your brain gets cluttered (fragmented), and it becomes harder to access and process information and make decisions.

You will find more examples of integrations and a list of correlations for experiences and feelings with underlying beliefs in my book, *Ending the Battle Within: How to Create a Harmonious Life by Working with Your Sub-Personalities,* which is available at Amazon.com.

Chapter 19

Release the Baggage

How can we free ourselves of past burdens?

What can we do when the upsetting events in our past are intruding into our lives today? Is there a way to clear the bad memories filled with sadness, anger, fear, and disappointment from our hearts and minds?

We may be remembering a breakup of a relationship, an accident, a failed project, loss of a job, or perhaps being taken advantage of by people who never return the favor.

The negative memory persists and creates stress until we finally reach our limit and want it gone. We need to release the weight of negative past events piled up in a mountain of sadness and regret.

This type of experience reminds me of a 1986 movie, "The Mission," set in 1740 in Paraguay. Robert De Niro plays Mendoza, a morally bankrupt Spanish mercenary.

While in Paraguay, Mendoza captures, murders, and sells the native Guarani into slavery, and his final violent act is when he kills his younger brother in a duel. With that brutal act, Mendoza spirals into depression, and a Jesuit Priest challenges him to undertake penance.

A particular scene that is so memorable to me is where Mendoza follows the Guarani natives as they climb up the side of a mountain next to a waterfall. Mendoza has a rope tied around his shoulders and is dragging his "penance," a massive bundle containing his armor, helmet, knives, and sword.

The baggage is pulling him backward as he climbs. He takes a few steps and then slides back down the muddy hillside. Again and again, Mendoza gets up and is barely able to move. He starts again to drag the heavy weight behind him.

Finally, his hands reach the top of the ridge, and he looks up. There is a Guarani brave with a machete held high over him. Mendoza puts his head down and is ready to die.

With one swift movement, the Guarani cuts the rope, and the baggage of weapons tumbles down the cliff into the water below. The tall native pulls Mendoza up onto the ridge, and together they follow the others into the forest.

This vision of releasing the baggage is a compelling example of letting go. The idea of cutting the rope and letting the baggage tumble down the side of the mountain makes sense. We all want to move forward without past burdens holding us back and weighing us down.

What can we do? There is a beautiful mediation that has helped me and others to cut the rope and let go.

It is called "The Rose Visualization."

Chapter 20

The Rose Visualization

Releasing negative events.

The Rose Visualization has served me and others to help release memories no longer needed or wanted in our minds. It was taught to me by Patrick McAnaney, a healer and psychic, who has a knack for making all things seem possible.

The following is the *Rose Visualization* with my embellishments that has worked well for me and others.

- **Imagine that you are walking up a pathway to a high plateau.** Wildflowers grow in open fields and under tall trees. You reach a quiet glen and in front of you is a large pane of clear glass, about 4 feet wide and 7 feet tall, held upright in a wooden frame.

- **Think of a negative experience that is bothering you.** It might be an accident, an illness, an argument, a complicated relationship, a divorce, a loss of a loved one, or any other challenging experience that made you feel sad, angry, or fearful. Imagine one of the scenes from that event. Place the picture of that scene onto the plane of glass.

- **Consider the scene.** Remember the impact of that event on your life and how it affected others. **Forgive yourself and others** who participated in this event. Say to yourself, "I forgive everyone involved and myself, and I let it go."

- **Now, place a white rose in front of the glass,** and drain the emotion from the scene into the rose that is changing from white to a variety of colors and begins to grow larger.

- **After all colors drain into the rose,** a black and white picture of the event remains on the glass. You have the choice to keep the black and white picture, or if you want to eliminate the experience from your memory, *break the glass.*

- **See the rose ascending high above you, drifting away.** Now blow up the rose that is filled with negative emotions. **Boom! It explodes** and color spreads across the sky.

- **Allow Love to flow through you** and feel that energy heal your heart, mind, and soul!

Now that you have let go of the weight and burden of an adverse past event and emotions, you will have more access to inner joy and peace.

Chapter 21

Emotional Health Flows in Balance and Harmony

Creating harmony in heart, mind, and spirit.

E motions flow like the wind through the trees. When we watch little children playing, we see them shift emotions. They can move from anger or sadness to giggling and romping in joy very quickly. On the other hand, what happens to the emotional patterns of teenagers and adults?

We tend to hold on tightly to our emotional response to what happens around us. Our memories and beliefs magnify our emotions, and we use proof from the past to build a case in our minds that reinforces our emotional behavior.

Is there a way we can create balance and harmony in our lives?

As you have read through this book thus far, you have found that there are techniques and Visualization you can use to shift your mind and emotions. By releasing negative memories and past events, you are creating an opportunity to welcome balance and harmony into your life.

What is Harmony? In music, it is described as a combination of musical notes that produce chords, which have a pleasing effect and a feeling of well-being. When music is inharmonious, it is called discord, meaning the sound is unpleasant and grates against our nerves.

Our reaction to disharmony is to be thrown off balance, Chaos and danger come to mind, and as a result, we block our senses to protect ourselves and become emotional.

Harmony and balance begin within ourselves. To be in harmony requires that we create a feeling of wholeness by living in truth and integrity. We need to speak authentically and keep our agreements with others and ourselves. Wholeness is balancing our work and entertainment, activity and rest, ambition and relaxation, and our materialism and spirituality.

Harmony is based on making peace with time, which means to live in the present moment. It is fine to learn from the past and then let it go. Work toward the future and relax into the present moment.

Expect and Accept Change. To stay balanced, we need to expect and accept changes in our life and in the world. Harmony is learning to live in the energy flow. As we continuously release and renew the old and create the new, we should be ready for exciting opportunities to expand our abundance, health, love, and joy.

Harmony is also *Grace*, which is defined as courteous goodwill and simple elegance or refinement of movement. Being kind and gentle can help move us into harmony with others and ourselves.

Happiness cannot be traveled to, owned, earned, worn or consumed. Happiness is the spiritual experience of living every minute with love, grace, and gratitude. — Denis Waitley

Harmony is the optimum state of being. It is *Balance, Equanimity, Moderation, and the Middle Way* (the Buddhist understanding of practical life, which is avoiding the extremes of self-denial and self-indulgence). *Emotional balance* is the ability to remain calm in the midst of turmoil. It is the ability to patiently and respectfully converse and work with others applying understanding and an open mind.

Living in Harmony begins by evaluating decisions
and determining if the choice to be made will lead
to confusion or clarity, harmony or discord,
turmoil, or peace.

Harmony and balance reconcile the extremes of opposing views and allow us to become lighter as we lessen our burdens and see the world from a much broader perspective.

Living in harmony is releasing the past so that our minds and hearts are open to the wisdom of the world and willing to listen and follow our Intuitive Guidance.

Today, as never before, we are engulfed in a unique period of transformation in which living in harmony with nature and our fellow human beings helps us create peace of mind, as well as improved health and well-being.

No person, no place, and no thing has any power over us, for 'we' are the only thinkers in our mind. When we create peace and harmony and balance in our minds, we will find it in our lives. — Louise Hay

Chapter 22

Blizzards of Energy

Recharging your life!

As we move through this current Blizzard of Energy, our beliefs, thoughts, and emotions are coming up for review. If we ride the waves and move above the blizzard, it may feel as if we are free-floating like a bird flying with the wind, higher and higher.

Experiencing the free-float is based on getting in touch with your Spiritual Center by moving your focus into your heart. It is crucial to rediscover talents and abilities and get in discovering your passions. You need to ask, "What brings me joy?"

Everything you focus upon will begin to manifest faster and faster. You will be amazed at how quickly physical items, people, and events will come into your life. It will feel as if you are riding on a down-hill bobsled, moving swiftly toward what you desire or fear.

Releasing memories and discarding the concepts that no longer serve you will allow Intuitive Guidance to present new opportunities. Letting go of past patterns of limitation and lack will enable you to soar.

You can become a Way-Shower and reveal to others what it's like to be happy and no longer caught in the crystallization of fear. It is exciting to demonstrate through your actions and attitudes that life is a grand adventure.

It is time to put your attention and intention on what makes you feel better, healthier, and more in touch with the real you. Forget about holding yourself back and become more active and expansive!

Be in the Moment. Live in the Eternal NOW!

Chapter 23

Positive Energy Transforms You

Are you ready to receive the transmission?

During this time of change, it is essential to gather and process positive thought-forms. Your mind is a receiver capable of accepting new concepts and ideas, and you can magnetize powerful thoughts of renewal, communication, and cooperation transmitted through time and space. You are capable of receiving inspiration, imagination, and creativity.

As you release thoughts that no longer serve you in terms of your work, purpose, and desires, you can expand into a broader perspective. The acceleration of the vibrational frequency on Earth is a transmission that purges the past and beams new information. As the frequency accelerates, it creates an incredible experience of change and transition.

You can help with the birthing of a new way of interacting with the earth as you join with those who have a similar interest in encouraging people to become more cooperative and aware. As human intelligence is activated, you will become more resourceful and capable of solving problems. You will receive visions for the future that can lead to renewing, revitalizing, and reinvigorating civilization.

The transmission is the inspired revelation of Universal Consciousness as it pours forth to those who are ready to receive and implement new ideas and ways of looking at their lives and the world.

You can participate by letting go of the past and opening to a new future. Some of the transmission will be garbled or misinterpreted, leading to mismanaged programs and projects. Find those people with practical experience and logical minds who are willing to stretch their thinking and begin working with the creative force to fulfill our mutual destiny.

Chapter 24

Universal Consciousness

Can you go beyond emotions?

Consciousness is being aware of our existence. It is our ability to feel sensations, experience thoughts, and make sense of our surroundings. It is also the very element of *knowing* about the world and beyond.

We can think of our minds and memories as if they are kept in a personal computer (our brains) with limited storage capacity. If you broaden your concept of awareness, you can imagine that Universal Consciousness (often referred to as God, The Creator, or All That Is) is similar to the World Wide Web, only more extraordinary.

Universal mind or universal consciousness is a concept suggesting an underlying essence of all being and becoming in the universe. It contains all that has ever been, all that is, and all that will be. We can tap into this *Knowing* because that broader awareness is actually within us. The understanding of universal consciousness is the elimination of separateness and any division in perception.

You usually operate your life based on limited consciousness, or you can open your awareness. You can welcome the

Universal Consciousness by turning your attention and relaxing into the connection with All That Is.

The question is, of course, "How do we accomplish this connection? What do we need to do to stay connected to the Source of All Information?"

First, you must quiet your mind and the thoughts that are trying to get your attention...all those voices moving through your head, telling you to do this or that and to hurry up and go here or there.

The following is a visualization you can do quickly and easily to quiet the mind in almost any environment.

Chapter 25

Dropping the Pebble Visualization

Clearing your mind.

S it in a comfortable chair with your back straight and both feet flat on the ground. Imagine you are sitting next to a small pond with clear water and a sandy bottom.

See yourself dropping a pebble into the pond, and it drifts down to the sand below. As the pebble drops, you feel yourself becoming calmer and more relaxed.

Then watch small bubbles rising from the bottom of the pond up toward the surface. Those are thoughts. Say hello to the ideas and let them go as they evaporate into the air. Drop another pebble and watch it drift down, down to the sand.

Each time the thought-bubbles rise to the surface, drop another pebble. Let the slow movement down into the pond take you deeper into the quiet, peaceful center of your being. Allow yourself to unwind in the knowledge that you are creating a new pattern of relaxation.

In this state, you are ready to hear, see, or feel the Divine Guidance available to you every moment of the day. You are open to Universal Consciousness.

After resting in this space for five to ten minutes:

- Bring your awareness back to this time and place.
- If you have time, write down any messages that might seem important.
- Move forward with a peaceful mind and heart.

Chapter 26

Four Cornerstones of Life

Health, Wealth, Love, and Self-Expression

The Four Cornerstones of Life provide the basis for a harmonious, joyful, and loving life. If any of the four cornerstones are missing, the building —your life—begins to tilt.

- **Health is first and foremost in importance to your life**. To participate and thrive in this swirling energy, you must take the time to care for your physical body.

- **Wealth is your medium of exchange** and the abundance that you experience in your life.

- **Love is your connection to others**. It is the basis of relationships in which you may share who you are.

- **Self-Expression is how you represent yourself** in the world—your way of expressing your inner self, creativity, and love of life.

Look at the elements of these Four Cornerstones and see where you might need improvement.

❖ Do you need better health? Do you need to lose or gain weight? Have you had a check-up with your doctor?

❖ How is the area of wealth in your life? Are your income, investments, and savings meeting your requirements?

❖ Is your special relationship loving, and is your interaction with family and friends satisfying and fulfilling?

❖ What is your mode of self-expression? Is it your career? Are you using your artistic abilities, such as decorating your home, gardening, painting, sculpting, pottery, collecting, music, or dance? Often self-expression is left out of our consideration, but it can be a significant part of what is missing in your life.

Chapter 27

Living Health

Can you love yourself unconditionally?

It is vital to love, nourish, and support our unique, earthly vehicle, our physical body. We have forgotten how elegant, sleek, powerful, and beautiful we are and can be. It is our love, caring, attention, and intention that maintains the physical representation of our spiritual essence.

We are Spiritual Beings manifesting in physical form on this plane of existence. We know that everything consists of energy, including our bodies. Our living, breathing physicality is continually renewing our bodies' cells, healing cuts, scrapes, and internal inflammation.

We are always in the process of accessing information from other people and the environment. We have the opportunity to experience and express our inspiration, creativity, talents, intelligence, and physical capabilities, which are outstanding in their diversity and complexity.

Everything we do profoundly affects our health: all that we believe, think, and speak, what we eat, when and how long we sleep, our exercise routine, playtime, type of work, and creative endeavors, all aspects of our lives.

With this increase in vibrational frequency, it is vital to balance our emotions. Intense stress and anxiety lead to anger that can shake up our body and create dis-ease.

What we eat can be helpful or harmful to our well-being. It is best to plan meals and eliminate snacks from our habitual routines. We need to take time to understand emotions, rather than unconsciously fill ourselves with sweets that add nothing but a *quick fix* to our lives.

To keep the body healthy and vibrant, avoid sugar in desserts and bread, toxins in alcohol and drugs, additives and preservatives in packaged and fast foods, hormones in animal products, and pesticides in fruit and vegetables.

Take the time and effort to learn what makes the body healthy, vibrant, mentally sharp, and emotionally relaxed.

We need to awaken our bodies' power and treat our physical form with increased respect and Love.

Chapter 28

Visualization for Health

Floating in the Sea of Tranquility

Imagine that you are sitting comfortably on a beautiful, white sandy beach looking out at the deep blue ocean. The sun has reached the horizon, and the sky is ablaze in glorious shades of red and gold, mirrored across the rolling waves of the sea.

Take a deep breath and relax to the seagulls' calls and the constant beat of the waves moving towards the shore. You stretch out your arms toward the sun and rise, standing tall, reaching toward the sky. You walk along the water's edge on the firm sand with the foam tickling your toes. You feel the expansive freedom and immensity of the Earth.

Your body, mind, emotions, and soul are in a unified state of peace and tranquility. Each movement is easy and comfortable. Your head is clear, and your heart is full of the Love you feel from the Universe. Your arms and legs and your torso float through the atmosphere, relaxed, yet strong and independent, yet connected to the wonder of being alive.

Every aspect of your Being is experiencing optimum health as you tap into the intense, Healing Flow of Love. You know that you are part of the Grand expansiveness of Universal Consciousness!

You open your eyes and know that you will heal quickly and easily from any dis-ease in your mind and body. You will guard your health by monitoring what you think, feel, and ingest to preserve your life and well-being.

You celebrate your health and vitality, knowing that you are young and vibrant, no matter your biological age. You laugh out loud, knowing that Infinite Love animates and energizes you now and forever.

Chapter 29

Enjoying Wealth

Is wealth more than money?

The second cornerstone is the medium of exchange for food, shelter, transportation, and interaction with other people. Throughout history, money has come in many different forms to buy and sell goods and services.

You would be wise to learn how to conduct business in a world based on economic activity. There is a good possibility that you have talents, abilities, concepts, and ideas that are valuable. No matter your capability, you have the opportunity to understand buying and selling so that you may live comfortably in the world.

Naturally, your service or product should fit or predict the needs or desires of the buying public. Your hobbies can become businesses, yet often you may need to use other talents to secure a job in the marketplace.

The concept of wealth goes far beyond money. For instance, when we view a fruit tree, we see hundreds of fruits bunched together on slender branches and are aware that *more than enough is the dominant theme of nature.*

Wealth can be an abundance in a number of areas of our lives. We can feel rich in loving relationships, creativity, travel,

95

exciting experiences, knowledge, perseverance, awareness of the beauty around us, and simply being grateful for the gifts we have already received.

Chapter 30

Visualization for Wealth

All of nature is abundant.

Imagine you are standing in a beautiful orchard with a variety of trees at the peak of their season. The scent of blossoms and fresh fruit is in the air as you gaze at the amazingly large oranges, lemons, and limes.

Inhale the fragrance of abundance and feel wealth around you. You know you are a part of nature, and Mother Earth has shown you that she always provides more than enough.

You smile as you realize that your life is your greatest gift, and you have the power to lift yourself beyond your current circumstances. See yourself making connections with people who can help and encourage you. The excitement of pursuing your dreams invigorates and gives you renewed strength.

In your mind's eye, see a vision of a home you would enjoy living in and a pleasant environment. What season of the year is it? Are there spring flowers? Do you feel the warmth of summer or are autumn leaves covering the ground? Do palm trees wave in a winter breeze or is snow falling past your window?

Imagine the people you are with and what you are doing. Are you swimming, hiking, or dancing at a party, exploring an historic city, or shopping at your favorite mall? You can enjoy any of these experiences by simply tuning into that vision in your mind.

Your creativity is endless, for you are a creator with your mind and heart. Change the scenario of your life by imagining new possibilities that can bring you joy!

The ability to vision is there for you to bring forward into your life. Forgive and let go of all the voices saying you cannot do it. Know that you can succeed. You have seen people live lives of fulfillment. It is possible. The road ahead beckons for you take the first step to create a new reality.

As you move forward, listen to and follow through with the guidance you receive. Be ready for synchronicities in which you arrive at the right place at the right time to meet the right person who is waiting for you on the path of life.

Now with renewed hope and optimism, open your eyes and be grateful for what you have and look forward to receiving the desires of your heart.

Chapter 31

Experiencing Love

Love is the highest emotion.

L ove is the Glue of the Universe. Love is the Creative Force that holds everything together. In other words, Love is God, and God is Love.

That Universal Love flows through you if you allow it. Messengers of God called Angels, which are aspects of that Force of Love, are continually working with you to provide guidance and support.

The more you allow yourself to relax into a higher vibrational flow, the more you will share in the wonder and glory of Love that lives in your heart, mind, and soul.

This all-encompassing Love is the same Love you feel for yourself, other people, animals, fish, fowl, and the Earth.

You are a receiver and broadcaster of the Love that animates you. Imagine that you are the center of a web of loving relationships, some near, others far. You have intimate relationships with family and close friends. Some people are merely acquaintances, associates, or slightly known. There are also many people you have only heard about or have seen in the media.

So, where does Love fit into all these relationships? Love is a deep feeling of affection and caring, creating a sense of oneness, leading to a desire to remain close and share your life.

Everyone has the opportunity to open their hearts to Love intensely and care about another person as much as they care about themselves.

Chapter 32

Visualization for Love

Love is the Only Answer.

You are sitting quietly in the shade on a garden bench surrounded by a profusion of colorful flowers. In front of you is a lovely pool rimmed by crystalline rocks that glisten in the sunlight. Golden coy swim round and round, streaming the surface of the water with wavering golden hues.

In the distance, you see a tall, pine-covered mountain with white fluffy clouds floating in a bright blue sky. You take a deep breath, focus on your heart, and feel it open to the beauty of the red and yellow flowers, the sparkling coy, the green mountain, and the blue sky.

You close your eyes, and a soft breeze caresses your cheek as you sense yourself surrounded by a golden-white cloud of Light and Love. This gentle cloud begins to move around your head, neck, shoulders, torso, and down and around your arms and legs.

Light and Love move down through your head and heart to the base of your spine, down through a grounding cord into the center of the Earth, clearing away any negative energy,

Slowly, you realize that Love and Light fill every cell of your body. You are the Light. You are Love.

The ever-present feeling of peace and joy, understanding, forgiveness, and Love fill your heart, mind, and soul!

As you take a deep breath, you open your eyes and know that you are loved far more than you could ever imagine.

Experimenting with Self-Expression

What are your talents and abilities?

How do you express your soul essence in the world? Few people in this time of upheaval are focusing on learning about their talents and abilities. The news and social media have taken over our lives. Films and series, documentaries, and exposés keep us entertained.

But what about you? Where are you in the midst of all the noise? How are you demonstrating creativity? How do you discover a sense of self in a world that promotes "stars" and drowns out you and the rest of humanity?

Self-expression is creativity and the expression of your feelings, thoughts, and ideas. You express yourself in conversation and your presentation to the world personally, socially, and professionally.

To express yourself creatively, you might choose writing, art, photography, sculpture, music, drama, dance, etc. In your professional life, you may enjoy education, healthcare, social work, science, developing a business, etc. You might delight in architecture, design, construction, sports, travel, adventures, philosophy, religion, politics, etc.

There are an abundance of ways to use the creative dynamics of your soul. You can experiment, play with materials, and use this time to examine which experiences bring you a renewed sense of purpose and a vital sense of worth.

Chapter 34

Visualization for Self-Expression

Creativity opens to receive guidance.

Imagine that you are walking through an enormous building with large windows and a very tall glass ceiling. Soft pastels cover the walls, and the floor is polished white stone.

This place is called the Cosmic Creative Center. Colorful partitions separate various studios where people are working on projects that will open new concepts and ideas for the world. They are exploring ways to develop their fullest self-expression without judgment or remorse.

You are in the Cosmic Creative Center to learn more about your talents and abilities. You are here to find out what activity or pursuit may have been missing in your life, so your days can feel more enjoyable and worthwhile.

Behind each partition are the necessary ingredients, all the materials you need to complete an art project, build your dream home, write a book, compose music, solve a scientific puzzle, or produce a movie, ballet, or opera.

Think about what you like to do. What types of books do you enjoy reading? What music makes you feel good? Have you looked at the wide variety of art, architecture, and interior design? Have you studied languages, cultures, and history?

You may realize that you have hidden talents that have been attempting to attract your attention. You might see that there are parts-of-you who want to express their individuality and creative ability.

You silently choose an area that looks intriguing and join others who are learning that skill. Time disappears as you indulge in the creative expression that fills your heart and emanates from your soul.

When you open your eyes, you see a new vision, a unique possibility to fill your days with the vibrancy of creativity and the essence of Love.

Chapter 35

Ten Steps to Self-Empowerment

Let yourself accept full power!

The word *Power* often is considered harmful because it implies a person who has control over other people. But *Personal Empowerment* means that we are taking the reins of our life, and we have the freedom to identify and define what we desire. We gain confidence to work with our hearts and minds to match the energetic frequency of what we wish to accomplish and who we want to be.

To be fully empowered, we must listen to our intuition and the wisdom of leaders and masters to steer our course. Our Guidance helps us to know when to take appropriate action to be in the right place at the right time. We are ready to make connections needed to fulfill our goals. More than likely, we will be surprised when we receive an even better outcome than we could have imagined.

The question is, can we feel empowered while we are in emotional turmoil? Probably not. Empowered means you feel strong, capable, energetic, and courageous. We have the added benefit of our Intuitive Guidance, which is protecting us, keeping us safe, and assisting us 24/7 to thrive and celebrate life.

Here are 10 Steps to Personal Empowerment designed to provide tools that will help us prosper.

This information may assist you in navigating and charting a clear course to your desired destination.

STEP 1

Forgive Yourself, Other People, and the World

We have pure light effervescence moving through us continuously. Yet, when grievances, anger, frustration, or fear block our vibrational field, it is difficult for Love and abundance to flow to and through us. Forgiveness releases the blockages and open our minds and hearts to receive.

It is essential to realize that we live in an imperfect world and that we are also flawed. We are not responsible, or are we the appointed judges of those imperfections. By forgiving ourselves, family members, friends, co-workers, and people in the news for all their mistakes or grievances we may have against them, we set ourselves free to enjoy life without dragging extra baggage along behind us.

Blocked enthusiasm stops our momentum. When our excitement and passion is held back, we lose the vitality that would otherwise be available to enhance our health and well-being. We can remove the obstruction and access our power easier by forgiving. Thus action can be channeled toward our goals and desires.

STEP 2

Take Inventory of What Is Real Versus Imagined

We need to reduce conflict in our lives by looking closely at reality. What are the personal boundaries in our lives that are preventing our movement forward? How many of these boundaries are real? Which ones are imaginary?

Fear is not real! FEAR is an acronym
For: *"False Evidence Appearing Real."*

Fear is composed of memory patterns re-created continuously by the mind that become bound within our magnetic core. This negative energy creates personal boundaries that restrict what we believe and limit what we can achieve. It makes our world smaller and less flexible.

It is crucial to learn the difference between fears and threats. Threats to our personal and economic safety and security can be real if based on authentic evidence rather than imagined outcomes. By knowing the difference, we are able to define our best course of action.

It takes a great deal of energetic resources to keep reinforcing imagined fears. Real threats require an immediate response to resolve or mediate them. We need to know the difference so we can broaden our personal and physical boundaries to create a clear path ahead.

STEP 3

Learn to Set Realistic Goals

Why do highly successful people always seem to be accomplishing much more in their lives? The answer is that they set achievable personal and business goals. It is vital to have a clear understanding of our unique skills and capabilities.

Setting realistic goals and achieving them dramatically reinforces and increases confidence and personal power. Desires and dreams may seem like motivating factors for the future, but sometimes concepts may be far beyond our current ability to make it happen. The difference between achievable goals and what we imagine in our dreams/desires can result in a continuous feeling of frustration, lack, and disempowerment.

When we evaluate our plans for the future, note that some of our training and ability may match our monetary goals. There also may be talents that are not income producing, yet as hobbies, they bring us joy. By recognizing the difference between goals, desires, and dreams, we will be one step closer to realizing self-empowerment.

STEP 4

Turn Off the Noise of the World

The world is a very demanding and dense field of forcefulness. We are a part of the world, yet we are each a unique human being. Just as no two snowflakes are alike, no two humans within the entire spectrum of humanity are entirely alike. The patterns of our Auric Energy Fields are particular to each of us.

It is impossible to assimilate all of the noise from media and technology that seems to demand our constant and full attention. By turning off the noise of the world, we have the opportunity to discover our true identity.

We can begin by taking a walk with our phones off, meditate, or listen to the silence in a quiet room. It is crucial to learn the difference between what the world is trying to sell versus what is essential for our consumption and satisfaction. Becoming quiet is necessary for our self-discovery and personal Empowerment to manifest our life goals.

STEP 5

Notice Signs, Indicators, and Confirmations

Signs, indicators, and confirmations are continually surrounding us within the matrix of the world in which we live. From scientific observation, we know that all things, alive or inanimate are composed of energy. Our vibrational fields manifest our life goals, and Intuitive Guidance is available to us every moment of the day.

Guidance is continually being sent to us to help
us learn, grow, and accomplish our mission in life.

Signs may come in a variety of ways. The form may be an experience of synchronicity, such as when someone we were thinking about calls. We notice an actual sign on a wall or read a paragraph in a book that gives us the information we need.

Indicators are further confirmation that we are on the right track and should continue. *Confirmations* are proof that the original signs and indicators were correct. As we pay attention to everything around us, we will see how the Universe is supporting us every step of the way.

STEP 6

Know Your Heart

Know your heart, and allow it to reveal your own unique and original design. Just as we have an individual perception and understanding of the world, so is our inner landscape of beliefs, thoughts, and feelings uniquely our own.

The human's energy center is the heart, which keeps us alive and serves as our emotional regulator. Our *awareness, personal understanding, and intuition emanate from our heart.* When we know our hearts, we open to understanding our purpose, motivations, inherent abilities, and reason for being.

It is essential to understand that our hearts are the central source of our energy. By following the energy stream from our heart to our mind and back again, we will experience renewed clarity, vision, and peace.

STEP 7

Living in the Moment Point of Now!

We are all travelers on the pathway of life. Each of us experiences our present moment based on our concepts of reality, experience, and expectations.

It is helpful to understand that our unique history need not be in charge of our lives. What has happened is completed, and our future is yet to be born. Instead, this breath, this scene, and these people are reflecting who we have become. We must stand strong in the *center point of our personal power* and decide what to do in this Now!

Lamenting failures and mistakes and voicing disappointment about opportunities missed will only keep us bound to the past. Our focus on what went wrong prevents our energy force from bringing into manifestation our heart's desires. *We re-create our past! Do we want our remembered problems to be the template for our future?*

We are growing wiser each day. Just as the baby becomes the child, the child becomes a teenager, the teenager grows into an adult, and we are being drawn into our real identity.

We must acknowledge our power at this moment and be inspired to imagine a rewarding, loving, and joyful future. Allow the Universal Consciousness and your intuition to guide you. Rest in the knowledge that you are One with All That Is.

STEP 8

Watch Your Words.

We all use words. We speak words casually, throwing them here and there at friends, family, and strangers. We make statements in "normal" conversations without thinking about the meaning or impact.

We write words in social media without much thought or consideration, sometimes blasting those we disagree with, using curse words with abandon. Or we bully, attack, or make snide remarks as if freedom of speech is the freedom to hurt someone deeply. The reality is that all of the words placed in sentences have meaning.

- Statements form images that activate emotions.

- Repeated statements create beliefs that solidify into your attitude and perception of the world.
- Those beliefs fed by emotion dictate your actions, which become your life.

Pay attention to what you say.
Each statement is a commandment.

Yes, the words we use become who we are. Or rather, our beliefs generate thoughts that affect our actions and form our personality and view of the world. When we use words of judgment or condemnation, negativity, or spite, these words all emanate from and return to the central core of our being.

Watching your words is one
of the most crucial steps to self-empowerment.

Using positive words creates a positive magnetic field. Conversely, negative comments create a hostile magnetic field. Quite simply, it is this energy field that ultimately magnetizes and manifests related events into our lives.

By watching your words and understanding that they are your commandments, you can shift your life and become who you truly are. You will change the future and manifest positive, empowering, fulfilling events in your life.

STEP 9

Listen to Your Inner Guidance

Self-Empowerment does not come from outside of you. Our power emanates from inside of us. When we acknowledge our uniqueness, only then will we form an identity that is truly our own. We will not need to continuously buy new and improved products or pay for more services to feel empowered.

Self-Empowerment is not power over anyone else. It originates in our radiant, energized, magnetic core, from which we receive perpetual guidance that matches our heart's desire.

Guidance comes in multiple forms
and is effortless and instantaneous.

It is essential to understand that Intuitive Guidance is broadcasted to us continuously and manifests through audio messages, signs or symbols, visions, dreams, a feeling or sensation, a hunch or "gut reaction."

Yes, there is such a thing as that *still small voice.* And that voice will speak to us if we listen and follow the guidance without delay.

To become genuinely self-empowered, we must understand and ultimately realize that this guidance is a significant part of our lives. We need to learn to trust our intuition implicitly, knowing that it is real, truthful, and always ready to protect and assist us throughout our lives.

STEP 10

Trust in All That Is

Trust in "All That Is" and know that self-empowerment is also a process of Self-Healing. A life that is joyful and self-realized with the desires of our heart is a life that is whole and complete. When we trust in All That Is, we are trusting in something far greater than the continuous calculations of our mental mind or ego for guidance and self-healing.

By listening to our inner guidance, that subtle voice, and being aware of signs, indicators, and confirmations manifesting in our life, we are trusting in All That Is to direct us to the matching template of our hearts' design.

The mental mind or ego is a wonderful tool,
but it doesn't know our true identity.

Who we are is a process of self-discovery and self-healing. The mental mind knows our past and projects our probable future based on past results. When we become a genuinely integrated spiritual being, we move far beyond the cognitive mind's limitations and heal ourselves through our joyful self-expression.

In this state of awareness and awakening, we will also help others on their path. We will be open to numerous probable realities, more than we can imagine. Self-empowerment and self-healing are natural partners in the complete expression of our life's journey.

Fall in Love with Life!!

About the Author

Verlaine Crawford has lived a wide variety of experiences, including being an entrepreneur, a marketing executive, consultant, publisher, author, speaker, and seminar leader.

Her marketing career included promoting healthcare, hospitality, retail, software, art, architecture, interior design, real estate, Chambers of Commerce, the American Cancer Society, and the AIDS Services Foundation.

Verlaine was born in San Francisco and when she was two, her family moved back to Iowa after WWII. She enjoyed an idyllic childhood, boating and ice-skating on the Mississippi River, gardening, and playing in the forest behind her home.

At the age of twelve, she and her younger brother, Roger, were mowing the lawn, and she didn't realize that he and his mower were behind her. She turned around, walked into the mower and cut both feet. She was in a wheel chair for a year.

And then her father left the family, and Mom, Elaine, decided to move her and Roger to Calif. They located in Carmel-by-the-Sea, CA, where she attended high school and then studied Political Science at U.C. Berkeley.

In 1967, aged twenty-three, she was introduced to metaphysics. It all started when she was in an elevator with a man who noticed that she was sad (a friend had suffered a heart attack). The stranger told her about his success making a list of the things he wanted and the dates by which they would happen and how it had worked perfectly. He gave her a book, "As a Man Thinketh" by James Allen and told her to make a list. She didn't learn the man's name and never saw him again.

She read the book and made her list. Everything on the list happened before the dates she had written. Within two months, she was modeling, appeared on a TV show, was working as an editor on *Keynotes*, the magazine of Capital Records, and living in a darling apartment in Belmont Shores near Long Beach. In 1968, she was able to go to Europe for three months; and after returning to Los Angeles, she met the man of her dreams in 1969.

This experience was the beginning of her exploration of how our thoughts create our reality. She used the information she gained from books, workshops, and intuitive guidance in her career and personal life. Many wonderful experiences came to pass, yet problems, health issues, and accidents did arise.

When she was twenty-seven in August 1971, Verlaine was in another room with elevators where she found herself in a frightening drama. It was in the underground parking of a fifteen-story building on the "Miracle Mile" in Los Angeles where she worked for an ad agency.

After she left the elevator and was heading for the door to the parking area, a man dressed as a guard grabbed her from behind and put a knife at her throat. When the other elevator opened with two men in it, her assailant stabbed her in the back, her lung collapsed, and the two attorneys came out of the elevator and saved her life. The "guard" escaped. For six months she worked with police to locate the attacker, but to no avail. She and John moved back to Carmel to begin a new life.

Five years later, it was at a seminar in Carmel about Neuro-Linguistic Programming that Verlaine received another piece in the puzzle of creating our reality. She learned the essence of the integration technique, which helped to explain how our hidden beliefs can create negative events and stop us from receiving our desires.

"I began teaching what I had learned because I wanted to share the information." Says Verlaine. "I felt everyone should know about how our beliefs are seeds that become thoughts, fueling our emotions, resulting in actions that create our lives."

In 1987, Verlaine's became aware of other Dimensions and began sharing what she learned with friends and people who came to hear what she had to say. John began a project in Europe, and they parted as friends.

In 1993, she married a doctor who was spiritual and lived in the mountain village of Idyllwild, CA. During the 1990's, she authored two books and was invited to teach spiritual seminars in Japan, Hong Kong, Australia, Bali, Europe, and across the U.S.

Verlaine's marriage ended after seven years in 2000. But fortunately, in 2001, she reunited with John Teressi, her first love and best friend for now over fifty years.

Verlaine currently keeps busy writing and is planning to do consultations on the internet and a podcast.

Verlaine's company, High Castle Publishing, has published (All the books are available on Amazon.):

Her award-winning, *Ending the Battle Within: How to Live a Harmonious Life by Working with Your Sub-Personalities. (Body, Mind, Spirit Mag Award of Excellence.)* by Verlaine Crawford.

Poetic Prose from visitation of an Angel: *Daughter of God: Angelic Messages of Wisdom and Love* by Verlaine Crawford.

The Heart of Transformation and the Butterfly Effect by Verlaine Crawford. Transforming your life to bring joyful experiences into your personal world

John Teressi's *Portals in Time: The Quest for Un-Old Age*, a fascinating fantasy, adventure novel that won eleven book awards and dozens of 5-star rave reviews.

The Alchemy of the Seven Harmonies by John Teressi. A gift book with photos of flowers and excerpts from the novel *Portals in Time.*

Websites: www.VerlaineCrawford.com
www.JohnTeressi.com
Contact at VerlaineCrawford@gmail.com.

Notes

List your talents and abilities?

What are your Heart's Desires?

How would you create a life of harmony?

www.ingramcontent.com/pod-product-compliance
Lightning Source LLC
Chambersburg PA
CBHW051834040426

42447CB00006B/517

* 9 7 8 0 9 9 9 8 0 3 6 6 0 *